How to Draw Horses

by Anna Betts

www.bsmall.co.uk

Contents

About the illustrations

The artist who put this book together has developed an advanced technique that uses a computer to add effects and colours to her drawings. This makes the illustrations really clear and easy to copy. If you do not have a computer at home then you can add colour by hand. In fact, this is what we expect you to do! Do not worry if your drawing is different to the ones in this book—they are your drawings.

How to use this book

The techniques in this book will teach you how to draw horses. The techniques get harder as you go through the book so start at the beginning to build up your skills.

By the end of the book, you will be drawing tall, strong and magnificent horses of all sizes.

There are a few skills that you will need before you can start some of the exercises.

Tracing
1. Place a piece of tracing paper over the drawing that you want to use.
2. Trace the outline of the image that you have chosen.
3. Turn the tracing paper over and scribble over the outline on the other side.
4. Then turn the tracing paper back over—the scribbled side should be facing down—and trace the outline again on to a piece of blank paper.

Copying
If the activity asks you to copy something then you can either trace it or you can draw it slowly on your own. You will need lots of practice to do this but if you observe the image carefully then it can be done.

Rubbings
1. Find a texture that you want to take a rubbing of. For example, wood, concrete or a wall.
2. Hold your paper against your chosen surface.
3. Using wax, a crayon or a colouring pencil, rub on the paper and the texture from the surface below will appear. You can do this on to a blank piece of paper or directly on to your drawing, if you are careful.

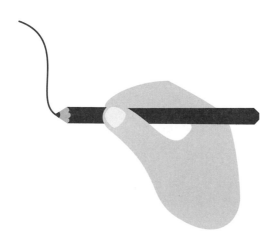

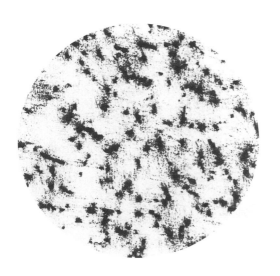

Curves

At first glance, a horse is a large, solid shape with a long back and straight legs. But, upon closer inspection, their body, legs and neck are full of gently curving lines and interesting detail.

1. This is a Dartmoor pony. Start by drawing the long, smooth back of the animal.

2. Gradually add the other curves to build up the body.

1.

2.

3.

4.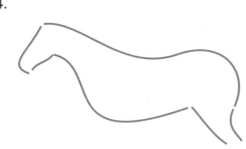

5.

6.

3. Once you have the basic shape, you can add details like ears, eyes, nostrils, a mane, a mouth and a tail.

4. You can now fill your pony with colour and patterns.

Tip: Ponies and horses look quite simple but this makes them difficult to draw because they are one large shape with very few colours on their bodies. The detail will help bring your creature to life on the page.

Negative space

Looking at the spaces between shapes, instead of at the shapes themselves, is a great way to notice all of the details. This area is called the 'negative space'.

1. Focus on the colourful part of the drawing below. This is the negative space around the horse. Using this space, you will be able to create the outline of the horse in the centre.

2. Starting from the edge of the page, draw straight lines towards the centre using a light pencil, like in the image below.

3. Using colouring pencils, create each colourful shape between the lines, one after the other, leaving the white part blank.

4. The horse will come together like a jigsaw puzzle. Now fill your horse with colour and patterns.

Tip: Choose a colour for your horse. Look at some photos to see the colours in their hair, manes and tails.

Circles

Groups of circles, ovals and other curved shapes can bring together the various details in a drawing of a horse. Look for circles within the large shape of a horse's body. Joining up these circles will guide your pencil and help to keep the shape of the horse.

1. Start with a circle for the head, one for the muzzle, and two for the body. Look at the position of the head, legs and belly.

2. Join the head and body with curves to make a neck. Draw the back and belly with more curved lines. Add the rest of the nose.

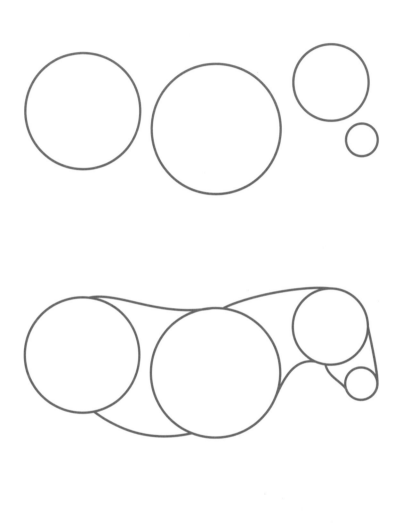

3. Now add the ears, legs and tail. Compare them to other parts of the horse to make sure that they are the correct size.

4. Once you have a good outline you can add more detail like the mane, nostrils and hooves.

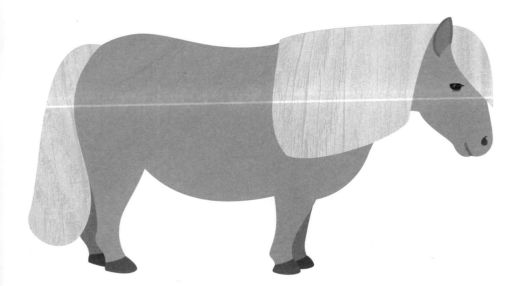

Scaling grid

A scaling grid breaks up an image into squares. Each square contains detail from the image. Working from square to square, you can copy the detail to another grid. Change the size of your image by using a bigger or a smaller grid, as long as it has the same number of squares.

1. Here is a grid of squares drawn over an image of a Danish Warmblood horse.

2. Copy the grid from the opposite page on to a blank piece of paper. See page 3 for instructions.

3. Look carefully at the horse on this page and start to draw the details on your grid using a pencil. Press lightly in case you need to rub anything out.

4. Think about the shapes made in each square by the horse's outline. Some squares will be blank and some will be full.

5. Once you have created the outline, rub out the grid lines and start to add colour. Draw in the details to your Danish Warmblood.

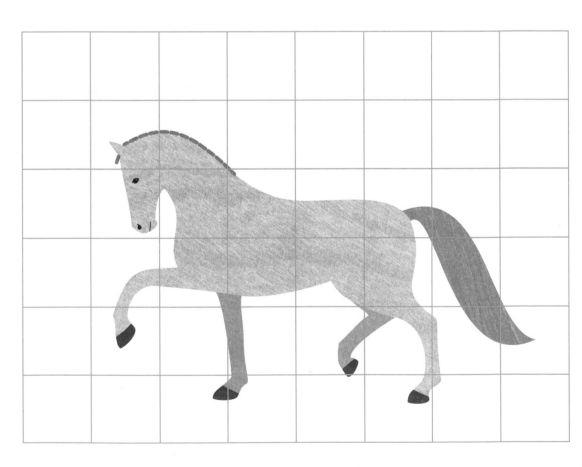

Materials

When drawing, the tools that you use are just as important as your technique. There are lots of pens, pencils and other drawing materials to choose from. You will need to think about what your picture needs.

Thickness

Thick lines are good for outlines and important features. Thin lines are good for detail.

Strength

Hard lines will suit still objects and soft lines will help to show movement.

Texture

Some tools make solid lines and others will create a scratchy effect.

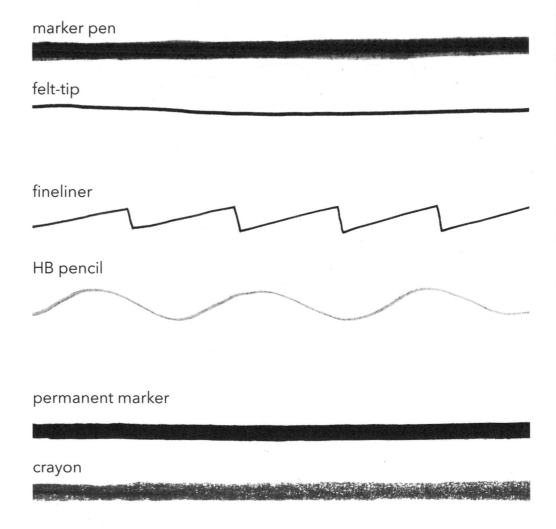

marker pen

felt-tip

fineliner

HB pencil

permanent marker

crayon

Colour

Colouring pens will look different to colouring pencils or even chalk.

The best way to learn about materials is to practise with them. Experiment to find out which tools give you the effect you want and which tools you enjoy using.

1. Trace this tail following the instructions on page 3.

2. Use different pens and pencils to draw over the outline.

3. Fill the shape with colour using pencils, pens or paint.

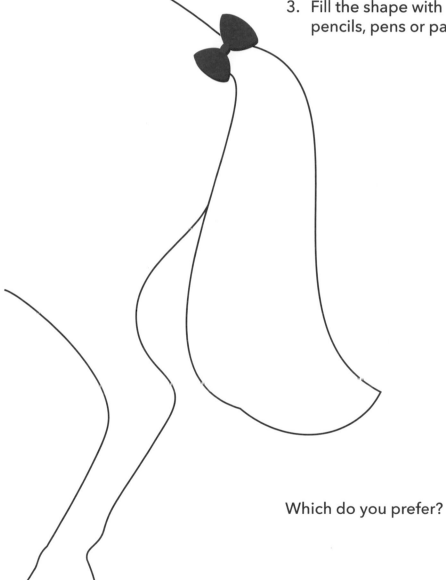

Which do you prefer?

colour pencil

colour felt-tip

colour paint

3D shading

Shading helps to make objects look more realistic. The shadows will be darker or lighter depending on where the light is coming from in your picture.

1. Trace or copy these shapes so that you can practise shading.

2. Choose the right kind of tool for the job. You will need a pencil.

3. There are three strengths of grey in these shapes: one light, one medium and one dark. The arrows show where the light is coming from. You can see that the side hidden from the light is darker.

4. For the cube, press gently with the pencil for the lighter areas and press heavily for the darker areas. Shade from side to side.

5. For the cylinder, shade from top to bottom on the sides.

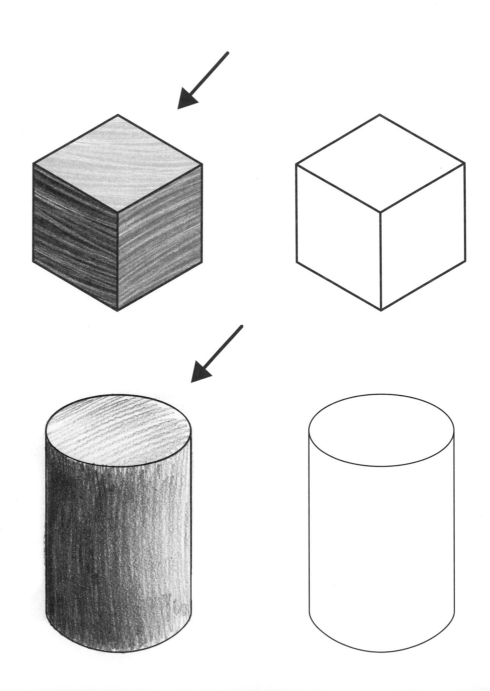

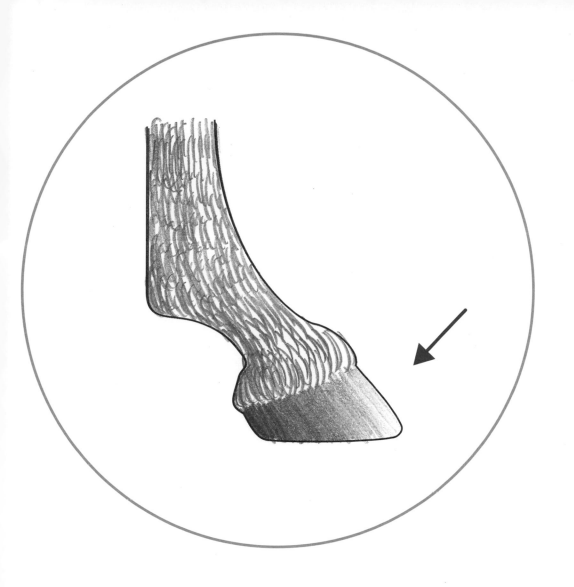

Once you have mastered the skill of shading, trace the outline of this hoof. Add the shadows. The red arrow shows where the light is coming from.

When drawing horses, the shading of the hooves is important because it is one of the few parts of the horse not covered in hair. The hooves will reflect the light differently.

Try moving the light source to the opposite side and then shading the hoof. Which side will be lighter and which side will be darker?

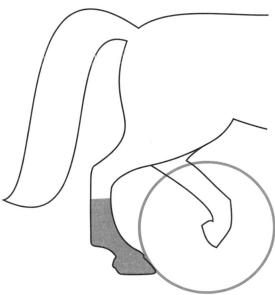

Geometric outlines

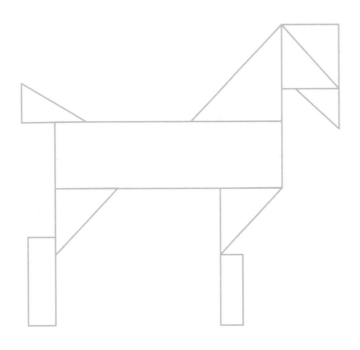

If a horse's body is not the right size when compared to its neck or legs, your drawing will look odd. By dividing up a horse into geometric shapes—such as triangles, squares and other shapes with hard corners—you can make sure these features are all the right size and in the correct place.

This technique is a useful way to draw a new type of horse for the first time. There are many ways to divide up an image with geometric shapes. Here are some examples to get you started.

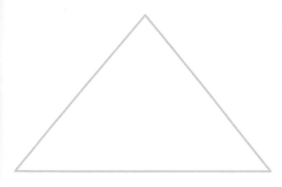

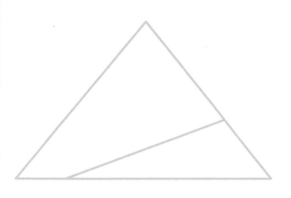

1. Copy the geometric patterns on to a blank piece of paper using a pencil. Press gently so that you can rub them out later.

2. Draw the details in and around the shapes. Use a different coloured pencil to help separate your drawing from the shapes.

3. Rub out the geometric shapes.

4. Draw in the details and add some colour to your horse.

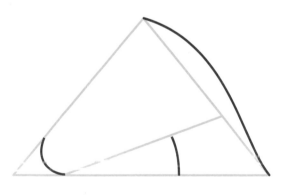

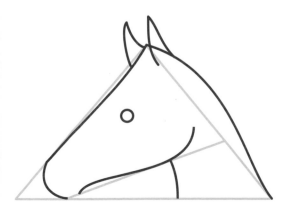

Patterns

There are many beautiful patterns in nature but horses are generally quite simple and plain. Zebra are very similar in shape to horses and have their own unique lines and stripes.

Patterns are attractive but difficult to create without careful planning. Here are some tips to help you bring some natural flair to your drawings.

1. Trace or copy the image from the opposite page.

2. Study the zebra's stripes. Look at the spacing between the lines and at the size of them. Curved stripes are more realistic and help to make the zebra look 3D.

3. Practise drawing the detail from the box on the right so that you are ready to add the pattern to the blank zebra.

4. Use a pencil to add the shapes before you add any detail. Make sure they are the right size.

5. Draw in the detail and add the black to complete your pattern.

Texture

swirly pencil lines

curved pencil lines

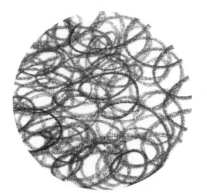

two directions

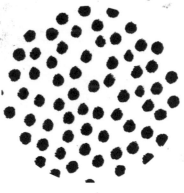

pen dots

piebald pattern

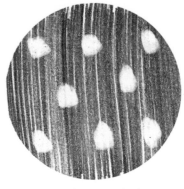

erased pencil dots

pencil dashes

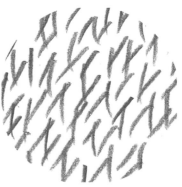

overlapping pencil dashes

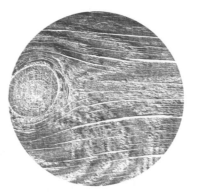

wood rubbing

There are hundreds of different textures that you can experiment with. Here are a few examples to inspire you. Since horses are quite plain when it comes to colour, these textures will help you to draw an interesting horse.

Create texture by using a variety of materials. Think about whether you need a smooth texture or a rough texture. This will make your horse drawing look more realistic.

Try to collect a page full of these different textures using the materials that you have. See page 3 for instructions.

1. Trace or copy this image.

2. Use the techniques on the page opposite to add texture.

Tip: Use one colour to create all of the textures on your horse drawing.

In motion

Horses are muscular creatures that can run at great speeds over long distances. They can even leap fences as they go. Drawing a horse in motion is an enjoyable and challenging task.

Here, you can see examples of horses galloping and jumping. The following steps will help you to create your own active horse.

1. Using a combination of the curves technique on page 4 and the circles technique on page 8,

or drawing freehand, start with the body of these horses. Pay attention to the angle of the body and the points where the legs join the body. These change with the horse's movement.

2. Study the neck, mane and tail of the horse. What position are they in? Add these details in.

3. The shading and textures you use can add movement. See pages 12, 14 and 20 for tips.

Use your imagination to make sense of your drawing. Is the horse running towards a friend or away from something scary? Why is the horse jumping?

Colour mixing

If you need a certain colour that you do not have, you can make it using the colours that you do have. You can use colouring pencils or paint.

Since horses are usually brown, black or grey, you will need to pay close attention to the shades. How dark is the brown on the mane compared to the leg, for example?

1. Draw the horse below using the techniques that you have already learnt in this book.

2. Study the different shades of brown. Find the dark browns and the light browns

3. Once you are familiar with the colours on the horse, practise making different shades of brown using these colour combination.

4. Add the colours to the horse and its surroundings.

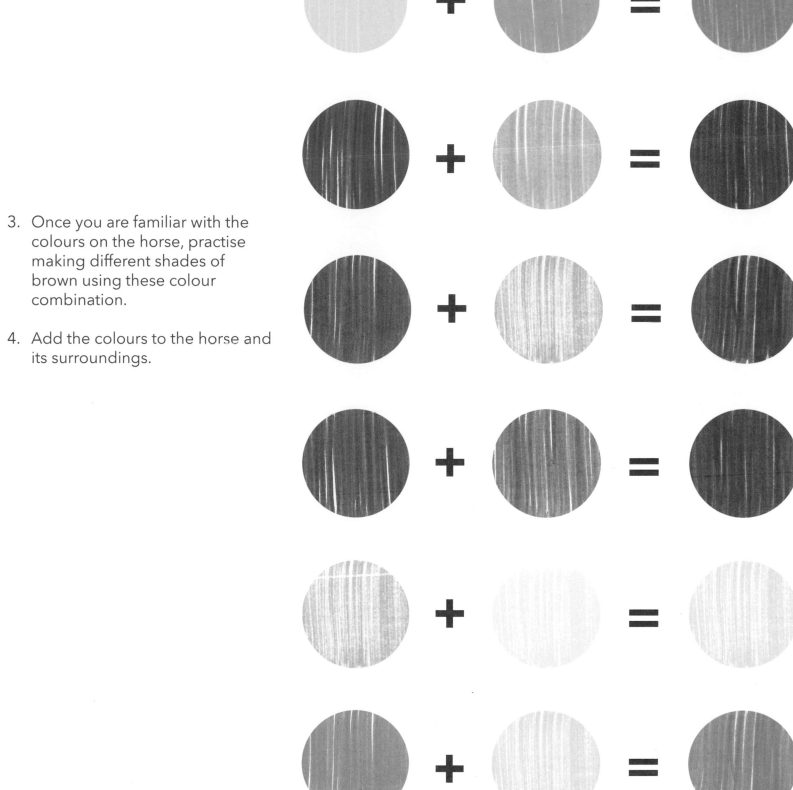

Line drawings

A line drawing is full of detail and has no colour. Lines will show the different parts of the horse such as the mane or the hair. For a technical drawing, you should use a thin, smooth line. You can read about adding character on page 28.

1. Work backwards from a colourful picture like the horse on the left of this page.

2. Look for the boundaries between the different colours and use a line to separate them.

3. Select an interesting detail such as the plait in the mane. Add lots of lines to show the layers of hair.

Plaited mane

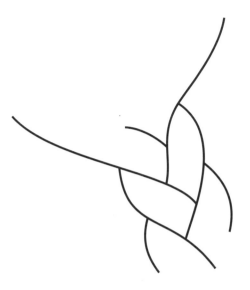

Trace or copy this
incomplete plait and finish
the pattern.

Drawing characters

Now is your chance to flex those creative muscles. Drawing a character is all about telling a story. Think about the main features of your chosen horse. This horse, for example, has long hair around his hooves that makes it look like he is wearing flared trousers.

1. Use a combination of the circles technique on page 8 and the curves technique on page 4 to create a line drawing.

2. Once you are happy with your drawing, add human features or clothing to make your character. The horse opposite is wearing disco clothing to go with his flared trousers.

3. Add facial features like a nice, big smile and give the horse some accessories, too.

4. Copy or trace the line drawing on the opposite page, or create your own, and have a go at coming up with more characters for your horses.

Once you have created your character, write a short story about him or her. What are they doing?

There are plenty of horses throughout this book that you could turn into characters. For example, the galloping horse on page 22 could be a spy or the pony on page 9 might make a good librarian.

29

Inspiration

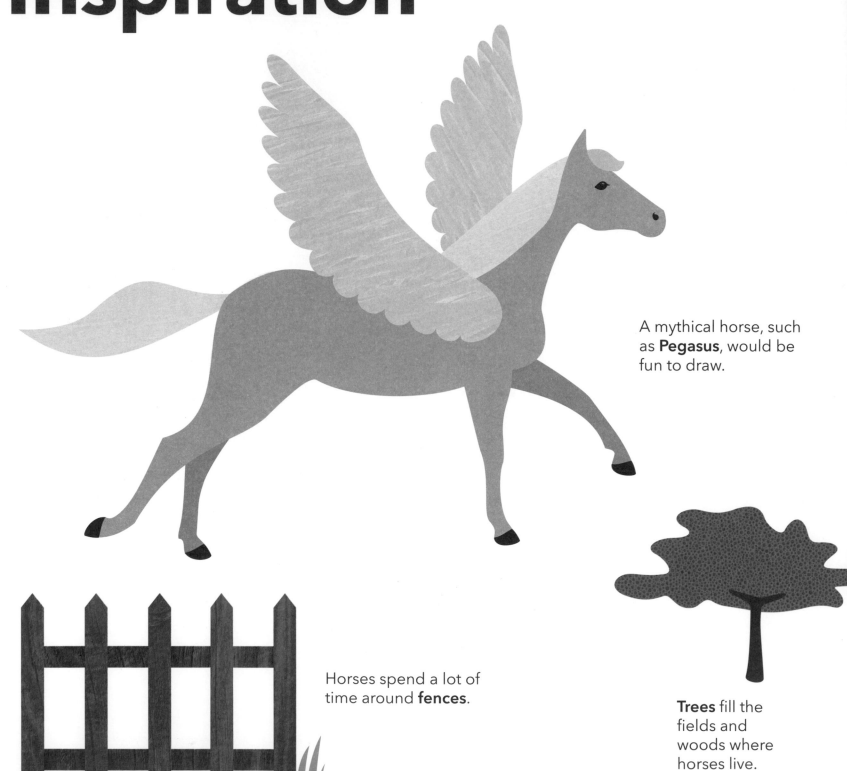

A mythical horse, such as **Pegasus**, would be fun to draw.

Horses spend a lot of time around **fences**.

Trees fill the fields and woods where horses live.

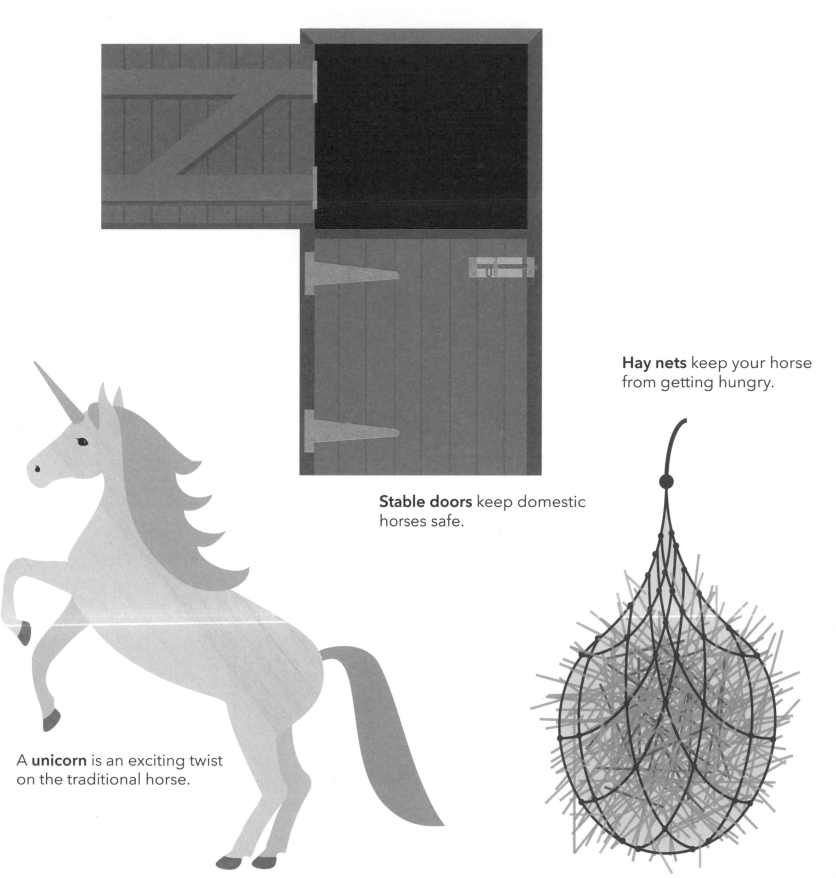

Hay nets keep your horse from getting hungry.

Stable doors keep domestic horses safe.

A unicorn is an exciting twist on the traditional horse.

Published by b small publishing ltd.

Text and illustrations © b small publishing ltd. 2016   1 2 3 4 5 6 7 8 9 10

British Library Cataloguing-in-Publication Data: A catalogue record for this book is available from the British Library.

Illustrations: Anna Betts   Design: Anna Betts   Editorial: Sam Hutchinson   Production: Madeleine Ehm

Printed in China by WKT Co. Ltd.   ISBN 978-1-909767-84-3

Please visit our website if you would like to contact us.

www.bsmall.co.uk